Leadership

SpiritBuilt Leadership 1

Malcolm Webber

Published by:

Strategic Press
www.StrategicPress.org

Strategic Press is a division of Strategic Global Assistance, Inc.
www.sgai.org

2601 Benham Avenue
Elkhart, IN 46517
U.S.A.

+1-574-295-4357
Toll-free: 888-258-7447

ISBN 978-1-888810-40-0

All Scripture references are from the New International Version of the Bible, unless otherwise noted.

Printed in the United States of America

Table of Contents

Introduction

This is the first of a series of books on leadership. Together, they comprise the series, *SpiritBuilt Leadership*.

This is not Leadership 101 (basic, motivational, anecdotal material with lots of sports and business stories) or Leadership 301 (advanced, academic, theoretical and focused). This is somewhere between the two. This is Leadership 201. In *SpiritBuilt Leadership* we will deal with basic conceptions of leadership with some "advanced" content.

The Goal

Our goal in *SpiritBuilt Leadership* is to help you move one or two steps higher than where you are now:

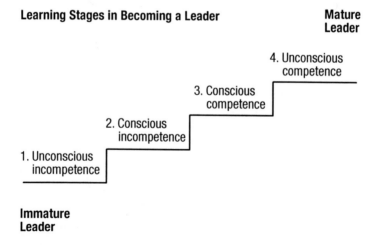

Learning Stages in Becoming a Leader   **Mature Leader**

4. Unconscious competence

3. Conscious competence

2. Conscious incompetence

1. Unconscious incompetence

Immature Leader

1. The first learning stage is where we all begin. At this stage of immaturity, we are unqualified and incompetent as leaders. However, we are largely unaware of how incompetent we really are. Sometimes we are even proud of our incompetence!

2. Through God's help, we grow to the second stage, where we first begin to realize just how incompetent and unqualified we really are. This marks the beginning of serious advancement, since we now know our need and begin to address it.

3. Through learning and experience, we reach the third stage of leadership – conscious competence. At this stage, we have grown in our qualifications and competencies as leaders. However, we are still quite conscious of what we must do and how we must do it. We are intentional and deliberate in our leadership.

4. Finally, at the stage of leadership maturity, leadership has become "second nature" to us. It comes naturally to us now. It is who we are.

The Process

If you put together a jigsaw puzzle, where do you start? Usually the four corners. They are easy to find because they have two straight sides. Then you look for the pieces with straight edges. Once you have connected all the straight edges, you will have the outline or framework within which you can put the other pieces together.

Much leadership teaching focuses specifically on issues in the middle of the puzzle, such as management, self-mastery, character, prayer life, envisioning, strategic planning, communication, power, delegation, motivation, persuasion, ethics, trust, mentoring, empowerment, team-building, decision-making, leading change, culture, creativity, etc. However, we must first establish the framework. That is the goal of this series.

In *SpiritBuilt Leadership*, we will put the four corners of the "puzzle" in place.

1. Leadership. What leadership is. The nature of leadership.
2. Leaders. What leaders are. The leader himself.
3. Leading. What leaders do. The practices of exemplary leaders.
4. Building leaders. How leaders are built.

Primarily, we will be sharing some conceptual frameworks and models. Our desire is to "demystify" leadership – to make it understandable and accessible.

There will also be some opportunities for guided reflection. When you do the exercises in the book, please go beneath the surface of your automatic reactions and be as honest with yourself as possible.

It will be most beneficial to study this book with others in a small group. That way you can learn and reflect together.

Our prayer is that this series of books will be effective in assisting Christian men and women around the world to be the mighty leaders God has called them to be.

Malcolm Webber, Ph.D.
Strategic Press
Elkhart, Indiana

chapter 1

What Is Leadership?

As a beginning, we will work on the basic definition of leadership: what is leadership?

Leaders have existed in all cultures throughout history. From Egyptian hieroglyphics, we know that symbols for "leader" existed as early as 5,000 years ago. Moreover, it is easily observed that leadership plays an important role in organizations of every kind. Without Joseph, the entire ancient world would have been destroyed by famine. Without Moses, the children of Israel would have remained in Egypt. Without Joshua, they would have remained in the wilderness. Without David, Israel would have been overcome by Goliath and the Philistines. Without Paul, the early church would likely have been deceived by the errors of the Judaizers. The Bible and church history are replete with the names of leaders who profoundly influenced the world. Similarly, the business world has its icons of leadership: men and women who took faltering corporations and turned them into spectacular successes. It is the same in every area of society; the worlds of religion, politics, education, sports, civil liberties and the armed forces all have their own heroes – those who society respects as "leaders." In particular, there is no shortage of leaders in the Bible – the greatest One of all redeemed us from our sins!

Because of its obvious importance, leadership has been a topic of great interest to historians and philosophers for thousands of years, but it was only at the start of the Twentieth Century that academic studies began. Over the last 100 years, scholars and writers have offered hundreds of definitions of "leadership." One American scholar counted over 350 definitions of leadership! It is likely that leadership is one of the most observed yet least understood phenomena on earth.

We know leadership exists and we know it is important. We know good leadership when we see it and we know when it is lacking. We know we *need* leadership. But what is it?

To you, what is leadership?

Before you continue, please take a moment, individually or in a small group, and write down your answer to this question. What is leadership?

_____

_____

_____

_____

_____

Or, think of how to demonstrate the meaning of leadership in a mime – by your actions without any words. Describe or act out a mime that would effectively demonstrate your definition of leadership.

Some current brief definitions of leadership are:

- Leadership is relationship.
- Leadership is influence.
- Leadership is vision.
- Leadership is transformation.
- Leadership is empowerment.
- Leadership is personal responsibility.
- Leadership is decision-making.

- Leadership is team-building.
- Leadership is change or managing change.
- Leadership is culture.
- Leadership is motivation.
- Leadership is persuasion.
- Leadership is creativity.
- Leadership is self-management.
- Leadership is communication.
- Leadership is character or integrity.
- Leadership is credibility.
- Leadership is trust.
- Leadership is modeling.
- Leadership is servanthood.

These are all good definitions of certain *aspects* of leadership but none of them is a sufficient definition of leadership overall. They are all too brief, too limited and inadequate.

The broad definition we will use in this study is:

A leader helps someone move from where he is now to somewhere else.

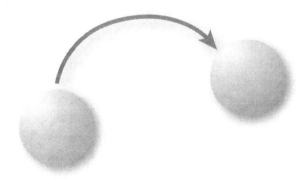

In addition, it is probably somewhere he would not go on his own. That is why he needs a leader. Leaders are necessary to do this: to help people move. People need leaders, or else they tend to stay in the same place.

Moses said to the Lord, "May the Lord, the God of the spirits of all mankind, appoint a man over this community to go out and come in before them, one who will lead them out and bring them in, so the Lord's people will not be like sheep without a shepherd." (Num. 27:15-17)

Jesus went through all the towns and villages, teaching in their synagogues, preaching the good news of the kingdom and healing every disease and sickness. When he saw the crowds, he had compassion on them, because they were harassed and helpless, like sheep without a shepherd. Then he said to his disciples, "The harvest is plentiful but the workers are few. Ask the Lord of the harvest, therefore, to send out workers into his harvest field." (Matt. 9:35-38)

Without leaders, people are like "sheep without a shepherd" – they wander aimlessly around accomplishing very little.

A leader helps someone move from where he is now to somewhere else.

Hopefully, the "somewhere else" is somewhere *better* than where he is now. This is one difference between a good leader and a bad one. Good leaders help people move to better places; bad leaders take people to worse places – they are effective leaders, but they are bad!

The lack of leadership is why so many people are not progressing in their lives. Many churches have great pastors, but many pastors aren't leaders. They are maintaining; they are taking care of the people in their church; but they are not *leading*. They are not helping their people to move anywhere. The people are only surviving; they are not fulfilling God's purposes. Certainly, the people do need to be taken care of but that is not enough. They also need to go somewhere. They need to mature and to fulfill God's purposes.

The scarcest resource in the church today is leadership capable of leading the people to fulfill God's purposes.

Why is there a lack of leadership in so many churches today?

- Many men in leadership positions simply don't have a leadership orientation or calling.
- Many men who are called as leaders are not sufficiently equipped in leadership.
- Many men who are leaders have no time for the future because they're too absorbed in the present.

Moreover, the lack of leadership is why many *businesses* stagnate. They may be good at what they do, but they are not keeping up with a business environment that is fast changing. Many businesses are being left behind – because of a lack of leadership.

The lack of leadership is also why many *families* do not fulfill the purposes of God for their lives. The lack of leadership is why *nations,* who are otherwise rich in resources, stagnate.

As a leader, you help someone move somewhere else. And essentially you help them move somewhere where they probably would not have gone by themselves. That is leadership.

Thus, leaders build bridges:

- From here to a better place.
- From the present to the future.
- From potential to fulfillment.
- From vision to experience.
- From anticipation to realization.

Leaders build bridges over the waters of impossibility.

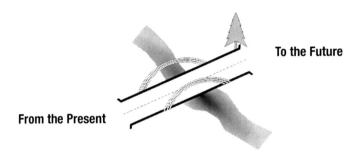

To the Future

From the Present

If there were only a few people who needed to move, then that few could swim. Boats could help a few more move from the present to the future. But if we want many people to make the move, we need a leader to build a bridge.

A leader helps someone move from where he is now to somewhere else.

Let's break this definition down:

A leader:
- This may be in any context – church, family, business, government, or education. Moreover, it may be at any level throughout an organization.
- The leader may be good or bad. There is both good and bad leadership. A good leader leads you somewhere good; a bad leader leads you somewhere bad. A leader leads you; he moves you; he takes you somewhere different from where you are now – that place may be either good or bad. Hitler, Stalin and Mussolini were all extraordinary leaders. They were very effective leaders. They moved many people great distances. However, they were bad leaders. Where they moved the people to was bad.

Helps:

- The good leader "helps" people move. He does not *make* them move. This is how he does it:
- The leader is at the front – calling to the people, "Look! Here's the vision!" "Here's where we can go!" "Here's what we can accomplish!" "Wow!" "Let's go!"
- The leader is behind – picking the people up when they fall, encouraging them, "You can do it!"
- The leader is beside – showing the way to the people, "Watch! Here's how to do it! Here's the path to walk in to get where we're going."

Someone:

- The leader must have followers. A person may be a great speaker, writer, scientist, inventor, musician or artist, but if no one is following him, he is not a "leader."
- These followers must be people. Leadership involves people. It is distinct from administrative paperwork, committee meetings, planning activities, or writing sermons.[1]

Move:

- Leadership involves movement; leadership involves change. Leaders must be willing to follow God when the "cloud" moves and to repeatedly let go of old ideas and old ways of doing things and adopt new and better ones. Moreover, they must be able to help their followers generate the high levels of enthusiasm needed to accomplish change. For the change to succeed, many people across the entire organization must move, but the leader is the one who often starts the movement or gives it direction and momentum.

In speaking of "change," we do not mean leaders will change orthodox doctrine or the eternal truths of the Word of God. Some spiritual leaders resist the idea of change because of their

---

[1] Many pastors would make quantum leaps ahead in their leadership if they would simply get out of their studies and touch people!

commitment to the unchanging Word of God. However, you can take a bottle of pure water and pour it into a variety of very different containers without the water itself being changed at all. In the same way, the eternal truths of God can be expressed in many ways and in many different forms. Sometimes, however, these forms become chains or straitjackets. They stifle us and make us ineffective in our ministries to others. It is these external forms – structures, processes, habits, ministry strategies, etc. – that God often wants to change.

From where he is now:

- The leader first understands where the people are now. Realistically, he examines the current state. He defines the *need* for change; he is not interested merely in change for its own sake. The leader must understand his people – their needs, conditions, circumstances, aspirations and capacities:

> *Be sure you know the condition of your flocks, give careful attention to your herds; (Prov. 27:23)*

The proposed change must serve the people, not merely the leader's own personal ambitions. Moreover, a good leader is deeply concerned with maintaining social harmony between the people throughout the change.

To somewhere else:

- After defining where the people are now, the leader then defines where they *could* and/or *should* go – the potential, the opportunity, the vision for the future or the solution to a major current problem. Then he defines *how* they will get there – the path, the broad plan. Then he says, "Let's go!" and leads them there. Along the way he encourages them to continue through the inevitable setbacks and disappointments until finally they reach their goal.

An All-Encompassing Definition

Our definition of leadership is:

> *A leader helps someone move from where he is now to somewhere else.*

This definition of leadership encompasses all the other short definitions we first mentioned:

- Leadership is *relationship*. It is a relational activity involving people. Leadership is not bookwork, budgeting or accounting – leaders interact with people, keeping healthy the social fabric of the organization. They maintain harmony as they help the people move and fulfill God's purposes.
- Leadership is *influence*. The leader influences people to make the move.
- Leadership is *vision*. The leader sees and then presents the compelling vision of where the move is to.
- Leadership is *transformation*. In the process of making the move, everyone involved is transformed.
- Leadership is *empowerment*. Good leaders empower the people to take responsibility and ownership of their move. Leaders believe in people and want them to fulfill their purposes in God.
- Leadership is *personal responsibility*. Rather than blaming problems and deficiencies on outside people, influences or events, the leader takes personal responsibility to move each person to take personal responsibility for the move to the desired future.
- Leadership is *decision-making*. Leaders have the courage and skills to make the many necessary, and sometimes hard, decisions regarding the move.
- Leadership is *team-building*. Good leaders realize they cannot do it all themselves; so they build an empowered team that will lead the people through the move. It takes a team to build a

bridge from the present to the future.

- Leadership is *change* or *managing change*. Leadership always involves change. This is the move itself – to somewhere better.
- Leadership is *culture*. Organizational culture is the set of shared beliefs, values and behaviors. This is how the leader leads – by shaping the organization's culture. This is one of the main things a leader does. The leader is a social architect. He designs and builds social fabrics within his organization. Think about your organization: what are the defining features of the culture of your organization? Those characteristics did not just fall into place by themselves. The leaders built this culture (whether intentionally or otherwise).
- Leadership is *communication*. It involves communication of the vision, the process and then encouragement and clarification all along the way. For communication to be effective, it must have three characteristics: clarity, passion and integrity. Clear communication will show the people where to go and how to get there; passionate communication will help the people want to go; integrity will mean they will trust you to actually follow you there. Without the ability to engage, convince, and inspire others – in large groups in public and also with individuals in private settings – leaders will find it difficult to enlist people in their cause.
- Leadership is *motivation*. The leader must motivate the followers or else they will never move. He should not do this through guilt, fear or force. The people should *want* to follow.
- Leadership is *persuasion*. Persuasion from the outside causes motivation from the inside.
- Leadership is *creativity*. The leader sees "outside the box." He sees new opportunities. He's not satisfied with the status quo. He creates new visions and new ways to achieve them.
- Leadership is *self-management*. The leader disciplines his own life to be able to fulfill his vision, and he leads his followers to do the same with their lives.
- Leadership is *character* or *integrity*. Christian leadership is

based upon integrity so the "where" and the "how" of the move will be appropriate.

- Leadership is *credibility*. People will only follow someone they believe in.
- Leadership is *trust*. Trust is integral to credibility.
- Leadership is *modeling*. Effective leaders do not merely "say"; they also "do" and thereby show others the way.
- Leadership is *servanthood*. Christian leaders should follow the example of Jesus. This is how the leader helps people move. Servanthood pervades good leadership. The heart of a true leader is to help his people become all they can be in God. The essence of servant leadership is seeking what is best for the followers in the purposes of God, and not oneself.[2]

The Three Parts of Leadership

Essentially, there are three parts to our definition of leadership:

1. The leader establishes the direction.
2. He aligns the people in that direction.
3. He motivates and inspires them to move in that direction and to fulfill the vision.

1. THE LEADER ESTABLISHES THE DIRECTION.

This is one of the primary roles of leadership. Good leaders are pioneers. They continually search for new opportunities to do what has never before been done. They are not content merely to maintain the status quo. Moreover, leaders see the great potential in their constituents, and want them to fulfill it. To do this effectively, the leader must be able to perceive not only the opportunities that are before the organization, but also the obstacles that stand in the way. Failure to do so will result in failed ventures and

---

[2] For more on servant leadership please see *Abusive Leadership: SpiritBuilt Leadership #6* by Malcolm Webber.

follies that discredit the leader and discourage his followers. Thus, leadership is more than just grandiose "visionary" talk. Anyone can "talk big." Remember the story of the boy who cried "wolf." After a while, no one believed him anymore. So it is with many leaders who continually cry "vision" when it is not realistic. After a while, no one believes them anymore. Good leaders have a vision that is realistic.

2. THE LEADER ALIGNS THE PEOPLE IN THAT DIRECTION.

After perceiving the opportunities, the leader must then translate them into organizational goals and enlist the people in achievement of those goals. The people must *clearly understand* and *personally own* the vision. This takes time.

Leaders who have spent months or even years developing their vision should not expect the people to "jump on board" the first time they hear it. They need time to understand it and to wrestle with its cost. In addition, the people are usually not as oriented to action and change as the leader is.

For any change there will be both risk and a price that needs to be paid. The people must count the cost and be willing to move.

A common error of visionary leaders is that they attempt to jump from establishing the direction to beginning to move toward its achievement. Visionary leaders must be patient with their people! They must effectively align the people first.

The primary instrument of alignment is communication. To be effective, communication must be clear, passionate and credible.

In this process of alignment, the leader must realistically assess his constituents' needs and abilities. Moreover, he must ensure that the vision is personally meaningful enough to his people to gain their commitment and effort.

As we will see, one primary difference between a good leader and a bad one is this:

- A good leader's vision serves the people.
- A bad leader's vision serves the leader himself.

3. THE LEADER MOTIVATES AND INSPIRES THE PEOPLE TO IMPLEMENT AND ACHIEVE THE VISION.

Once the people genuinely share the vision, they must be led in its implementation and fulfillment. This requires role modeling on the part of the leader (Heb. 13:7). He must demonstrate his total dedication to the cause he shares with his followers – even to the point of accepting personal risk and making self-sacrifice for the good of the organization (Phil. 1:29-30). He must also empower the people by giving them genuine responsibility as well as the authority to fulfill that responsibility. Finally, the leader must continually encourage them to keep moving in the right direction (Phil. 1:6; Gal. 6:9).

EXERCISE

Please find examples in the Bible of the three parts of leadership.

ONE EXAMPLE

Look at the three parts of leadership in Jesus' Great Commission:

> *Then Jesus came to them and said, "All authority in heaven and on earth has been given to me. Therefore go and make disciples of all nations, baptizing them in the name of the Father and of the Son and of the Holy Spirit, and teaching them to obey everything I have commanded you. And surely I am with you always, to the very end of the age." (Matt. 28:18-20)*

Jesus established the direction. He shared a clear and compelling vision with His disciples:

- *make disciples of all nations*
- *teaching them to obey everything I have commanded you*

Jesus had already aligned His followers in that direction through what He had already taught them:

- *everything I have commanded you*

Now He aligned them in the specific direction He wanted them to go and said, "Start moving…":

- *go and make disciples of all nations, baptizing them in the name of the Father and of the Son and of the Holy Spirit, and teaching them to obey everything I have commanded you*

Finally, Jesus motivated and inspired them to keep moving and to fulfill the vision:

- *surely I am with you always, to the very end of the age.*

ANOTHER EXAMPLE

Nehemiah was a mighty leader in the Old Testament who led the children of Israel to rebuild the walls of Jerusalem. First, Nehemiah saw the vision. As he was serving King Artaxerxes as cupbearer, Nehemiah heard that the walls of the city of Jerusalem had been broken down and its gates had been burned (Neh. 1:3). Going before the Lord, Nehemiah wept and interceded for his people (1:4-11), and God gave him a vision to return to Judah and rebuild Jerusalem (2:5).

Now that Nehemiah had the vision, he began aligning the people with it. The first person who needed to own the vision was King Artaxerxes. As Nehemiah came before the king, he stated his case clearly and passionately. "If it pleases the king," he pleaded, "and if your servant has found favor in your sight, I ask that you send me to Judah, to the city of my fathers' tombs, that I may rebuild it" (2:5). The king granted Nehemiah's requests, sent letters of recommendation to the governors of the area, and gave him timber from the king's forest as well as soldiers (2:7-9). King Artaxerxes had caught the vision! Once Nehemiah arrived in Jerusalem, he went before the people and shared his vision, explaining the damage to the city and the plan for rebuilding it (2:17-18). When the people heard him, they embraced the vision and began to work (2:18). The plan was in motion!

Then Nehemiah kept the people moving toward fulfilling the vision. Each family was given a portion to repair and soon the wall was "half its height, for the people worked with all their heart" (4:6). There were some who sought to attack and destroy the city, but Nehemiah, not deterred, encouraged the people to continue laboring, half of them building and half of them bearing arms (4:15-18, 20; cf. 2:20). Despite setbacks and conspiracies against Nehemiah, he did not give up. They "continued the work with half the men holding spears, from the first light of dawn till the stars came out" (4:21). Nehemiah's leadership was effective. After only fifty-two days of work, the wall was completed (6:15) and God was glorified (6:16)!

OTHER EXAMPLES

Moses: in Exodus 3, Moses received the vision from God (part 1). Then he shared the vision with the people (2). Finally he led them out of Egypt and through the wilderness, overcoming many obstacles until they finally reached the Promised Land (3).

Joshua: in Joshua 3, Joshua had received the vision of crossing the Jordan and entering Canaan from Moses (1). Then he aligned the people with that vision in verses 2-4 (2). Finally he led them across the Jordan into Canaan in verses 5-17 (3).

Jethro: in Exodus 18, Jethro had a vision for a better system of government within Israel (1). He shared the vision with Moses, aligning him with it in verses 14-23 (2). Then Moses, motivated by Jethro, implemented the vision in verses 24-26 (3).

David: in 1 Chronicles 17, David received the vision from God to build the temple (1). He shared this vision with the people so effectively that they willingly brought everything necessary for its construction in 1 Chronicles 29 (2). Then Solomon actually built the temple beginning in 2 Chronicles 3 (3).

Leadership is a Collage

Even though we speak of its three parts, leadership is not a simplistic step-by-step procedure of moving through a series of predictable and successive points. In reality, leadership is a complex *collage*. It is an experiential collage of diverse people, tasks, responsibilities, pressures, duties, deadlines, opportunities, crises, blessings, sufferings, rejections, successes, mistakes, etc., with no clear way of making sense of it all or of immediately-apparent prioritization or path to accomplishment.

Leadership is hard. It can be complicated. But with God's help, you will succeed!

Leadership in Every Context

Our definition of leadership encompasses every context in which leadership occurs.

> *A leader helps someone move from where he is now to somewhere else.*

In *church* leadership, the leader leads the people God has entrusted to his care (1 Pet. 5:2) into spiritual maturity, and the fulfillment of God's purposes, in which every member is a minister and the people of God know God, love one another and reach the world for Jesus.

In leadership in the *home,* the father leads his wife, children and extended family into spiritual maturity, and the fulfillment of God's purposes so that everyone in the family fulfills his potential – intellectually, academically, socially and spiritually.

In Christian leadership in *business,* the leader leads others – including the people working for him, his suppliers, customers and competitors, and the surrounding community – into the glory of God so that his business is a wonderful witness to the Lord Jesus, and so it takes care of the people in it, achieves profitability and provides a genuine service for the community.

EXERCISE

Please be as specific and clear as possible as you answer these questions.

1. Think of a good leader you know about.

   Who was the leader? _____

   Who did he or she lead? _____

   Where did he or she lead them to? _____

   _____

   What can you learn from this example? _____

   _____

2. Think of a bad leader you know about.

   Who was the leader? _____

   Who did he or she lead? _____

   Where did he or she lead them to? _____

   _____

   What can you learn from this example? _____

   _____

3. Think of a time in your own life when you were an effective leader to someone.

Who did you lead? _____

Where did you lead them to? _____

_____

What can you learn from this experience? _____

_____

_____

_____

4. Apply this now, either individually or in your leadership team, to your life and/or ministry (focus on your goals and not so much on the process of accomplishing it at this point).

Who are you leading? _____

Where are you leading them to? _____

_____

How can you do it better? _____

_____

_____

_____

The "Fly-On-the-Wall" Envisioning Exercise

Imagine that your wildest dreams concerning your organization are about to be fulfilled. Then imagine you're a fly on the wall looking at your organization in five years time. You're watching what is happening at that time.

Step 1   What do you see?

As much as possible, forget about the present and think entirely about the future. What does it look like? What is happening? Describe the details of what you see. Only when you have clearly seen the future – totally removed from the present – move to the next step.

Step 2   Now think back from the future and, painting with broad strokes, think about the kinds of processes, systems, strategies and structures that brought all this to pass.

Step 3   Now move to the present and consider how to connect the present with the intermediate processes, systems, strategies and structures that will be necessary in order to bring your vision to pass in the years to come.

This is considerably more difficult than it sounds. This is "backwards-thinking." Most people find this exercise extremely hard to do – especially at first. It is an uncomfortable inner discipline to entirely break away from the present and simply allow oneself to dream about the future. But until we do this, we will always be bound in our thinking by the limitations and constraints of the present – all the reasons why we can't do something. God's realm is the unlimited!

If you will do this exercise, you will find it liberating and effective. It will help you to actively pursue God's strategy to achieve His purposes for the future, instead of doing what many leaders do:

- Only ever thinking ahead from the present to the future and thus making merely incremental improvements.
- Being led by circumstances and reacting to them, instead of proactively planning the future.
- Copying someone else's good idea. So many leaders simply follow the herd doing whatever is currently popular.

Step 1.   Forget the present. Define the future.
          What does it look like?

Step 2.   Painting with broad strokes, how did it happen?
          Think back from the future.

Step 3.   Connect the present with the necessary processes to bring the future to pass.

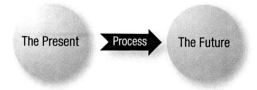

An Example of This Three-Step Process

Step 1   A leader has a long-term vision of his own church helping the church in other nations mature and accomplish more effective ministry. He sees his own church doing this specifically through sending materials and teachers.

Step 2   The broad strategic process for this to happen includes focusing on one nation at a time, then producing materials, training teachers, building relationships and credibility with leaders in the target nations, raising finances.

Step 3   In prayer, choose the first "target nation." Determine what materials are needed there; start producing or finding them. Begin training teachers. Take first trip to the target nation to begin building relationships. Begin to present a vision for this to the constituents to raise finances.

chapter 2

Are Leaders Born or Made?

For years, people have debated whether leaders are born or made. We can identify four main schools of thought:

1. The "born-leader" idea. This approach asserts that genes are the major forces behind leadership. You are either a "born-leader" or you are not. Since the "right genes" are relatively rare, effective leaders are too. Of course, we all know that some people are "born leaders": leadership comes very easily and naturally to them.
2. The "early childhood" school. According to this view, the most important factor in whether someone becomes a leader is his early childhood development. Since the "right family" is also rare, great leaders are too.
3. The "gifted-leader" school. This view contends that leadership is a supernatural gift that is only given by God to a few.[3]
4. The "life experiences" idea. According to this belief, leadership is learned through experiences. Consequently, we can almost "create" leaders simply by giving them the right training or exposing them to the right life experiences. (This is a very popular view today.)

---

[3] We do agree that there are particular leadership giftings that God gives only to some (not all) in the church (e.g., Rom. 12:8, Eph. 4:11). Our present context, however, is much broader, encompassing every kind of leadership – in the home as well as in business, education, government, etc. When viewed in this broadest sense, leadership – to some extent – is in all of us. As noted earlier, one of the purposes of this study is *to "demystify" leadership*: to make it accessible to all of us – not only the select few that have the special, indefinable "something" called leadership that the rest of us can never aspire to.

To you, what is the right answer?

Before you continue, please take a moment, individually or in a small group, and write down your answer to this question. Are leaders born or made? Which of the four views is right?

_____

_____

_____

As you probably already realize, a balanced position would accept that *all* people have untapped leadership potential – to some degree. There are clear differences due to nature (i.e. genes) and nurture (i.e. early developmental experiences in life) as to how much untapped potential there may be in a particular individual. Furthermore, there is no doubt that the experiences of life (such as work experiences, hardships, opportunities, education, role models and mentors) all go together in the crafting of an individual leader. Moreover, the specific calling and gifting of God differ from person to person.

However, no matter what level of leadership ability a person currently demonstrates, he or she can make quantum improvements.

Leadership is in all of us. With learning and practice we can all do better.

This is not to suggest that everyone is called to be an "organizational leader" such as pastor or business executive – someone with a formal, positional status of "leader." We all have very different callings (1 Cor. 12). However, there are several pervasive *kinds* of leadership:

- Personal leadership. We are all called to take responsibility for our own lives, moving ahead to fulfill God's purposes.
- Family leadership. The parents – in particular, the

father – are the God-appointed leaders of the family.

- Relational leadership. At certain times, we are all called to take responsibility for helping others move ahead in their own lives.
- Spontaneous leadership. There will be times in almost everyone's life when sudden circumstances require that we lead others in certain ways.
- Organizational leadership. This is the formal role of leadership.

Thus, while we are not all called to be formal, "organizational leaders," there are many contexts in our lives in which we all are, nevertheless, "leaders."

EXERCISE

Review your life and think about a leadership success that you have enjoyed. Think about one time in high school or college, at work, at home, in your neighborhood or community, on a sports team, or in a church group, when you made something good happen through other people that would never have occurred without your leadership. Think about a time when you helped someone move to a better place. This should represent a kind of "personal best" on your part.

It did not have to involve a time when you were the formal or official leader, although it may have. You may have simply emerged informally in some context as a leader.

It can be in any setting – but it must involve other people.

It can have happened at any time in your life.

Some personal examples from my life:

1. When I was a boy, my family owned a canary. Regularly, when its cage needed to be cleaned, the bird was allowed to fly around inside the house. One day when the cage was being cleaned, the bird escaped out of the house. I gathered some friends and neighbors together and formed a search party to search the neighborhood for our canary. Although the bird was spotted high in a tree, we were not able to recover it. Nevertheless, I had exercised leadership in the rescue effort.

2. I was once invited to assume leadership of a very unhealthy church. In the process, I started a new church with those who wanted to join me. Thus, I led two leadership efforts at the same time: a turn-around initiative for those who were already involved in the old church, and the birthing of a new church. Although we endured some very tough times, in both regards, by the grace of God, my leadership efforts were ultimately successful.

Once you have a clear picture in your mind of a time of leadership success in your life, tell the story to the people in a small group that you're a part of. As a group, reflect on what made the leadership successful, and then generate a list of the characteristics of effective leadership built on your experiences.

As you describe the important qualities of leadership, you will realize that you know what effective leadership is all about. You may also realize you haven't exercised it for many years.

Thus, even if you feel like you're not a leader, you have the capacity to be a leader nevertheless. Leadership is not some mysterious and elusive quality accessible only to a few.

You've done it once so you can do it again!

Knowing this, you should:

- Be open to your own leadership potential.
- Be challenged to improve in your leadership.
- Be motivated to develop other leaders.

chapter 3

Why Do People Follow You?

Let's review our definition of leadership:

> *A leader helps someone move from where he is now to somewhere else.*

But how does a leader get the people to move? Why do the people want to follow the leader?

What is the basis of the legitimacy of his leadership?

Please complete the exercise on the following page, before you proceed.

EXERCISE: WHY SHOULD PEOPLE FOLLOW YOU?

For this exercise, think of a present leadership position you hold and respond accordingly. If you do not hold any formal leadership positions, then imagine you did have a position that you would like, and answer accordingly.

You are a leader. You have followers. You expect them to follow you. Why? Why should they follow you?

Put a 1 beside the reason that most closely represents the main reason why you expect people to follow you. Then rank the other reasons in order of importance: 2 is the second most important reason why people should follow you, 5 is the least important.

_____ I have the power to punish those who don't follow me. That's why people should follow me. (#1)

_____ People follow me because they want to. They genuinely like me as their leader. (#2)

_____ God has appointed me as the leader of these people. They should recognize and respect this fact and follow me. (#3)

_____ Those who follow me are doing the best thing for themselves because they will be rewarded in some way – either by me or by God. (#4)

_____ I am the most qualified for this task of leadership. Therefore, people should follow me. (#5)

Five Kinds of Power

A leader helps someone move from where he is now to somewhere else. We may define leadership "power" as the leader's *capacity to influence others to move* from where they are now to somewhere else.

There are essentially five reasons why people follow someone else, or five kinds of "power":

1. Coercive power.
2. Reward power.
3. Positional power.
4. Expert power.
5. Servant power.

We will look at each of these kinds of power in detail.

1. COERCIVE POWER.[4]

This means the leader has the ability to administer punishment in some form to those who don't do what he says. Such a leader uses the fear of punishment to motivate his followers.

This kind of leadership is sometimes found in (often small) churches in which an insecure pastor maintains his following by threats, such as "if you leave this church, you will lose your salvation (or, at least, your place in God's end-time move, etc.)!"

Sometimes this power can degenerate into sheer brute force. The political leaders of Jesus' day used this kind of power to rule. Military dictators use this to get the job done. One national leader said, "Political power is obtained from the barrel of the gun." Today, some religious cults use physical violence to gain a following.

---

[4] This was answer #1 in our initial exercise.

41

In some situations, the fear of punishment is legitimate. For example, an employer has the authority to fire someone who doesn't fulfill his obligations. Therefore, the employees follow their leader's directions. Moreover, a parent needs to establish this kind of authority early in the life of his small child. That is quite legitimate.

Furthermore, there are a few times when this is appropriate in the context of the church. For example, the prospect of church discipline is a legitimate motive for sinning members to repent:

> But now I am writing you that you must not associate with anyone who calls himself a brother but is sexually immoral or greedy, an idolater or a slanderer, a drunkard or a swindler. With such a man do not even eat. (1 Cor. 5:11)

> For even when we were with you, we gave you this rule: "If a man will not work, he shall not eat." We hear that some among you are idle. They are not busy; they are busybodies. Such people we command and urge in the Lord Jesus Christ to settle down and earn the bread they eat. And as for you, brothers, never tire of doing what is right. If anyone does not obey our instruction in this letter, take special note of him. Do not associate with him, in order that he may feel ashamed. Yet do not regard him as an enemy, but warn him as a brother. (2 Thess. 3:10-15)

Additionally, God chastens His children so they obey Him:

> because the Lord disciplines those he loves, and he punishes everyone he accepts as a son. (Heb. 12:6)

Furthermore, the fear of God's future judgment is a legitimate motive for people serving Him now:

...The fear of the Lord – that is wisdom, and to shun evil is understanding. (Job 28:28)

...be afraid of the One who can destroy both soul and body in hell. (Matt. 10:28)

For we must all appear before the judgment seat of Christ, that each one may receive the things done in the body, according to what he has done, whether good or bad. Knowing, therefore, the terror of the Lord, we persuade men... (2 Cor. 5:10-11, NKJV)

In general, however, coercion is not an appropriate kind of power for Christian leaders to use.

not lording it over those entrusted to you, but being examples to the flock. (1 Pet. 5:3)

The following table sums up key aspects of the use of coercive power.

Coercive Power	
Benefits	Costs
Can be effective for gaining obedience	Drains physical, emotional and spiritual energy from both leader and follower
Appropriate for disciplinary actions	Undermines positive attitude of followers
Achieves quick results	Destroys trust and commitment
	Becomes less effective over time (must be repeated with greater and greater force)
	Obedience obtained by this means is usually only superficial, and often grudging
	This process must be supervised continually
	Followers may respond in kind! Leaders who live by the sword will likely die by the sword
	The use of such power is usually not biblical

2. REWARD POWER.[5]

In a corporation, if you do what your boss tells you to do he might promote you to a higher level, or he might give you extra pay for working overtime. Consequently, you obey him. At school, the students who desire the reward of good grades will work hard. This is reward power at work.

This also is appropriate in the Christian life sometimes. For example, the promise of future rewards is a legitimate motive for faithfulness now:

---

[5] This was answer #4 in our initial exercise.

If what he has built survives, he will receive his reward. (1 Cor. 3:14)

If I preach voluntarily, I have a reward... (1 Cor. 9:17)

For we must all appear before the judgment seat of Christ, that each one may receive what is due him for the things done while in the body, whether good or bad. (2 Cor. 5:10)

Rejoice and be glad, because great is your reward in heaven... (Matt. 5:12)

...and your Father, who sees what is done in secret, will reward you. (Matt. 6:18)

...store up for yourselves treasures in heaven, where moth and rust do not destroy, and where thieves do not break in and steal. For where your treasure is, there your heart will be also. (Matt. 6:20-21)

Peter answered him, "We have left everything to follow you! What then will there be for us?" Jesus said to them, "I tell you the truth, at the renewal of all things, when the Son of Man sits on his glorious throne, you who have followed me will also sit on twelve thrones, judging the twelve tribes of Israel. And everyone who has left houses or brothers or sisters or father or mother or children or fields for my sake will receive a hundred times as much and will inherit eternal life." (Matt. 19:27-29)

and into an inheritance that can never perish, spoil or fade – kept in heaven for you, (1 Pet. 1:4)

However, the rewards that the Bible encourages us to look forward to are always *eternal* rewards. When material, temporal rewards are used as incentives, they frequently become stumbling blocks to one's motive (cf. 2 Kings 5:26). I knew of a ministry that planted a new church in a foreign country. The leaders found it very hard to get anything done, so they began to pay the new believers to do various things for them. After a while, it became impossible to get any of the local Christians to do any kind of ministry unless they were paid to do it!

> ...men of corrupt mind, who have been robbed of the truth and who think that godliness is a means to financial gain. But godliness with contentment is great gain. (1 Tim. 6:5-6)

> Be shepherds of God's flock that is under your care, serving as overseers – not because you must, but because you are willing, as God wants you to be; not greedy for money, but eager to serve; (1 Pet. 5:2)

The laborer *is* worthy of his hire (1 Tim. 5:18), but this should not be his *motive* for serving. Much damage has been done to churches by leaders who continued in church leadership only because they were not sufficiently skilled or qualified to work in a regular job for a living; the sole reason they remained in spiritual leadership was that it was their only way to have an income.

Thus, reward power in the materialistic sense is not appropriate for most forms of Christian ministry.[6]

The following table sums up key aspects of the use of reward power.

---

[6] There is an exception to this. Jesus affirmed the use of *increased responsibility* in this life as a reward that would motivate faithfulness (Luke 16:10).

Reward Power	
Benefits	**Costs**
Sanctioned in certain cultures, such as the U.S.	Undermines the real "want to" in followers; motives for service become mixed; creates stumbling blocks
Focuses attention on group priorities – "we pay for what we want"	Does not consistently produce high performance. "I'm only paid to do 'thus-and-so' and no more!"
Effective for gaining obedience – temporarily, at least	Undermines commitment if rewards are perceived as insufficient
Boosts short-term performance	Churches, and other nonprofit ministries and groups, have limited tangible rewards to offer
	Many organizations are too complex for clear reward systems
	Temporary – giving a reward may ensure short-term success, but not long-term commitment
	Expensive – one must provide increasingly greater tangible rewards
	Ineffective if rewards are not desirable or attractive
	Destructive if wrong individuals are rewarded
	Destructive if partiality is practiced
	Encourages self-centered individualism
	Ignores the reality that Christians are not primarily driven by material incentives
	Is not biblical in most situations. Jesus requires us to give up our lives in this world

Taken together, the coercive and reward strategies form the "donkey" approach to leadership: leading by means of a carrot (reward) and a stick (coercion). One problem with this strategy is that if you treat people like donkeys they will start to act like donkeys!

> *Do not be like the horse or the mule, which have no understanding but must be controlled by bit and bridle or they will not come to you. (Ps. 32:9)*

3. POSITIONAL POWER.[7]

This kind of authority resides in the position rather than the person. In other words, "I'm the leader, so you must follow me." This is the organizational equivalent of "because-I'm-the-Mommy" power.

A new factory owner went to lunch at a nearby restaurant which featured a "blue plate special" that allowed for no substitutions. When he asked for a second piece of butter, the waitress refused. Irritated, he called for the manager, but she also refused him. "Do you know who I am?" he asked indignantly. "I am the new owner of the factory across the street." The woman smiled and said, "Do you know who I am, sweetie? I am the person who decides whether you get a second piece of butter." The power of positional authority!

There are times when the use of positional power is appropriate. For example, people should obey police officers simply because they are the authorities. Similarly, school teachers, parents and employers should all be obeyed whether or not they're absolutely right about something. You may disagree with your boss about how to do something,[8] but you should do it his way nevertheless – simply because he's in charge.[9]

---

[7] This was answer #3 in our initial exercise.
[8] In an appropriate way, of course.
[9] Assuming he's not asking you to do something that would constitute sin (Acts 4:19-20; 5:29).

Everyone must submit himself to the governing autho-rities, for there is no authority except that which God has established. The authorities that exist have been established by God. (Rom. 13:1)

Children, obey your parents in the Lord, for this is right. "Honor your father and mother" – which is the first commandment with a promise – "that it may go well with you and that you may enjoy long life on the earth." (Eph. 6:1-3)

Positional power may be appropriate at times for church leaders – usually when someone who is contentious needs to be reminded who is "in charge." There are also times when the leader has to make the final decision on a difficult issue, and the people should respect that decision simply because he is the leader.

However, positional power should not be the main reason why church leaders expect people to follow them. This was the kind of leadership that the Pharisees exercised:

Everything they do is done for men to see: They make their phylacteries wide and the tassels on their garments long; they love the place of honor at banquets and the most important seats in the synagogues; they love to be greeted in the marketplaces and to have men call them "Rabbi." But you are not to be called "Rabbi," for you have only one Master and you are all brothers. And do not call anyone on earth "father," for you have one Father, and he is in heaven. Nor are you to be called "teacher," for you have one Teacher, the Christ. The greatest among you will be your servant. For whoever exalts himself will be humbled, and whoever humbles himself will be exalted. (Matt. 23:5-12)

Essentially, the better the leader, the less he needs to rely on positional power.

The following table sums up key aspects of the use of positional power.

Positional Power	
Benefits	**Costs**
Sanctioned in certain cultures, such as Mexico and the Philippines	Lowers performance. People only cooperate when the "boss" is around
Puts the weight of the entire organization behind the leader	Lowers followers' commitment and "want to"
Effective for gaining obedience	May become less effective over time
	Becomes very complicated in a multicultural situation
	Creates distance between the leader and the people. Positional leaders encourage "distance" through their clothing, titles, etc.
	Weakened by any display of weakness, failure or simple "humanity" in the leader
	Puts pressure on the leader to be "perfect" and to always have the right answer
	Can become difficult for the leader to have genuine nurturing friendships with others
	Mitigates against transparency and accountability of leadership

4. EXPERT POWER.[10]

This is based on the person and not on the position. Experts are influential because they supply needed information or skills. They have the credentials. People follow them because they know what they're doing. They have particular knowledge or skills that qualify them for the task.

Certainly, Christian leaders should know what they're doing:

> *He must manage his own family well and see that his children obey him with proper respect. (If anyone does not know how to manage his own family, how can he take care of God's church?) (1 Tim. 3:4-5)*

> *Do your best to present yourself to God as one approved, a workman who does not need to be ashamed and who correctly handles the word of truth. (2 Tim. 2:15)*

However, this is not sufficient reason to expect others to follow – simply because you are the "smartest" person around. The following table sums up key aspects of the use of expert power.

---

[10] This was answer #5 in our initial exercise.

Expert Power	
Benefits	**Costs**
High commitment and "want to" in followers	Takes a long time to develop deep credibility
High performance in followers	Must possess the necessary knowledge and skills
Drains little, if any, spiritual and emotional energy from leader	Not as effective in gaining quick compliance as the first three forms of power, particularly in the case of disobedience
	May not be effective if followers do not share the leader's goals

5. SERVANT POWER. [11]

This is when people will follow you because they respect you. It's not because you demand respect; it's because you have earned it. People follow you because they want to follow you.

It's not just that:

- They will be punished if they don't.
- They will be rewarded if they do.
- They must because you're in charge.
- They think you know what you're doing.

But they admire you, they like you, they love you, they respect you. They *want* to follow you.

If you are a leader God has raised up then you will want this to be the primary reason why people follow you.

---

[11] This was answer #2 in our initial exercise.

A servant leader sets people free. He wants people to follow him because they genuinely want to. This means the followers will have adequate knowledge of alternative leaders and alliances and the capacity to choose among those alternatives. People will *freely* respond only to leaders who are proven and trusted as servants.

Servant leadership is a relationship based on personal influence. Another kind of leader may think of himself as a boss, but a servant leader will see himself as a coach or facilitator – one who serves others. Jesus calls us His "friends" (John 15:15)!

This kind of leadership influence depends on feelings of affection, esteem and respect. This loyalty is nurtured over a long period of time.

The differing source of power is one of the key distinctions between servant leadership and the leadership of the world. If you take away a leader's formal position, credentials and ability to reward or punish, will the people still choose to follow him? Servant leadership truly depends on who you are rather than on your position, title, knowledge, or ability to give rewards and punishments.

Servant Power	
Benefits	Costs
High commitment and "want to" in followers	Takes a long time to develop
High performance in followers	Not as effective in gaining quick compliance as the first three forms of power, particularly in the case of disobedience
Biblical basis for leadership power	Requires death to self and personal sacrifice

53

How Jesus Led

Jesus led His followers by means of servant power.

- As God, Jesus *could* have immediately punished everyone who wouldn't follow Him. (Coercive power.)
- He *could* have offered them great wealth, fame and success in this life if they would follow Him.[12] (Reward power.)
- He *could* have simply said, "I'm in charge – in fact, I'm God – you must follow me!" (Positional power.)
- He *could* have appealed to His infinite wisdom and knowledge of all things – "I'm the smartest one around so you should follow me. I know what I'm doing." (Expert power.)

All four kinds of power would have been appropriate and right for Jesus to use. Instead, He served His followers.

> *Jesus called them together and said, "You know that the rulers of the Gentiles lord it over them, and their high officials exercise authority over them. Not so with you. Instead, whoever wants to become great among you must be your servant, and whoever wants to be first must be your slave – just as the Son of Man did not come to be served, but to serve, and to give his life as a ransom for many." (Matt. 20:25-28)*

> *They came to Capernaum. When he was in the house, he asked them, "What were you arguing about on the road?" But they kept quiet because on the way they had argued about who was the greatest. Sitting down, Jesus called the Twelve and said, "If anyone wants to be first, he must be the very last, and the servant of all." (Mark 9:33-35)*

Who is the greatest? The one who is the servant. This is Jesus' master principle of leadership. Because He served His followers, they loved and respected Him and *wanted* to follow Him even to the point of death (Matt. 26:35).

---

[12] In spite of the claims of the "prosperity Gospel," Jesus actually did not offer His followers this. He did, however, offer them persecution and tribulation!

Please read John 13:3-17 – another of the great servanthood passages. We can gain some insights into the true nature of servant leadership from this passage:

- Servanthood is not weakness.

> *Jesus knew that the Father had put all things under his power, and that he had come from God and was returning to God; (John 13:3)*

Jesus' servanthood was not out of personal weakness, but personal strength. He knew who He was in God. He knew He was God. He was very secure in who He was.

Only those who are secure in Christ can exercise true servant leadership. Those who are insecure become dominating and possessive, ambitious and competitive. They intimidate others through their expertise, manipulate them through coercion or reward, or dominate them through position.

- Servanthood must be chosen.

> *so he got up from the meal, took off his outer clothing, and wrapped a towel around his waist. (John 13:4)*

Jesus chose this style of leadership. No one made Him do it – no one even expected it! He could have chosen the other kinds of leadership.

In reality, few men choose this style of leadership:

> *I have no one else like him [Timothy], who takes a genuine interest in your welfare. For everyone looks out for his own interests, not those of Jesus Christ. (Phil. 2:20-21)*

Moreover, servanthood must be chosen daily. It is not a one-time event. We must take up our crosses daily, allowing God to put to death our own agendas and ambitions.

- Servant leadership is genuinely selfless.

> *After that, he poured water into a basin and began to wash his disciples' feet, drying them with the towel that was wrapped around him. (John 13:5)*

> *...he knew who was going to betray him... (John 13:11)*

How many pairs of feet did Jesus wash? 12! Jesus knew Judas was going to betray Him, yet still washed his feet. This reveals the selfless nature of true leadership. The true Christian leader will not only serve those who can benefit him or who are assured of succeeding in the future. The godly leader will also serve those who he knows will let him down – even those who he knows will stab him in the back! He serves not only the loyal but also the disloyal; not only the strong but also the weak; not only those with great potential but also those without apparent potential.

- Servanthood does not mean weakly letting everyone else set the agenda.

> *"No," said Peter, "you shall never wash my feet." Jesus answered, "Unless I wash you, you have no part with me." (John 13:8)*

Jesus' servanthood did not mean that He gave up being in charge, and just naively let others set His agenda for Him. He was always the leader. Servant leadership is not "people-pleasing" but doing the will of God.

> *"You call me 'Teacher' and 'Lord,' and rightly so, for that is what I am." (John 13:13)*

To be a servant does not mean you don't lead, but it establishes your motive for leading and your attitude as you do lead. Some think that true servant leadership means that you give up leadership and let others set the course and the agenda. Servant leadership does not mean you *give up* leadership. It refers to the motive, style and the attitude with which you exercise your leadership. You must lead, but you must lead *as* one who serves.

The Characteristics of Servant Leadership

The following are some essential and biblical characteristics of servant leadership:

- Our model is the Lord Jesus who "did not come to be served, but to serve, and to give his life as a ransom for many" (Mark 10:45).
- In the Kingdom of God, greatness is ranked by service, primarily through voluntarily being last (Mark 10:43-44).
- One of the primary functions of leaders is to serve the needs of others. The leaders serve the people (2 Cor. 4:5); the people do not serve the leaders.
- If you have a heart of servanthood towards people, they will follow you. You won't have to flash your badge of authority at them, to let them know who they're supposed to take their orders from. People will want to follow you. They will respect you and trust you and want to follow you. You will become their role model:

  > To the elders among you, I appeal as a fellow elder, a witness of Christ's sufferings and one who also will share in the glory to be revealed: Be shepherds of God's flock that is under your care, serving as overseers – not because you must, but because you are willing, as God wants you to be; not greedy for money, but eager to serve; not lording it over those entrusted to you, but being examples to the flock. (1 Pet. 5:1-3)

- This kind of relationship with the people takes time to nurture. The first four kinds of power are quicker and easier to use.[13] The true servant leader must build a life before the people that earns their respect and trust. Thus, churches that change pastors every 3-4 years are destined to perpetual fruitlessness, as are the leaders who try to lead them.
- This relationship must continually be re-charged. Just because you served someone 10 years ago, and they wanted to follow you then, doesn't mean they still do now. This must be a continual lifestyle of leadership.
- We do not start with servanthood and the cross and then move on to "bigger and better things." We start in servanthood and we go deeper and deeper in servanthood and in the cross.
- Servant leadership always results in people following Christ, not the servant. This is because ultimately – and in the truest sense – we're all serving Him. Consequently, the servant leader will not be guilty of the arrogant self-promotion that characterizes so many insecure religious leaders today.

> *Are we beginning to commend ourselves again? Or do we need, like some people, letters of recommendation to you or from you? (2 Cor. 3:1)*

> *For we do not preach ourselves, but Jesus Christ as Lord, and ourselves as your servants for Jesus' sake. (2 Cor. 4:5)*

The servant spirit of Jesus is revealed in Isaiah 42.

> *He will not shout or cry out, or raise his voice in the streets. (Is. 42:2)*

Jesus was not a self-promoter. Neither should we be.

---

[13] The first three, in particular, can be *immediately* successful when used. Coercive, reward and positional power *take* authority; servant power *earns* authority.

- Servanthood involves stewardship:
- Of the gifts that God has given you. This means the servant leader will use his gifts for the benefit and advancement of others and not himself.

> *Each one should use whatever gift he has received to serve others, faithfully administering God's grace in its various forms. If anyone speaks, he should do it as one speaking the very words of God. If anyone serves, he should do it with the strength God provides, so that in all things God may be praised through Jesus Christ. To him be the glory and the power for ever and ever. Amen. (1 Pet. 4:10-11)*

- Of the people you serve. This means your desire will be to mobilize and empower them to find their greatest fulfillment in life and ministry (Eph. 4:11-13). This also means the servant leader will be sympathetic with the weak and merciful and understanding toward those who err. This was the spirit of Jesus. For example, Jesus served Peter and restored him when he fell.

> *A bruised reed he will not break, and a smoldering wick he will not snuff out. In faithfulness he will bring forth justice; (Is. 42:3)*

- Servanthood involves self-giving even to the point of death if necessary. The servant leader must be totally dedicated to the cause he shares with his followers – even to the point of accepting personal risk, personal loss and self-sacrifice for the good of others.

> *I am the good shepherd. The good shepherd lays down his life for the sheep. (John 10:11)*

> *men who have risked their lives for the name of our Lord Jesus Christ. (Acts 15:26)*

- The servant-leader is the one God will anoint and vindicate!

> *Here is my servant, whom I uphold, my chosen one in whom I delight; I will put my Spirit on him and he will bring justice to the nations. (Is. 42:1)*

> *Whoever serves me must follow me; and where I am, my servant also will be. My Father will honor the one who serves me. (John 12:26)*

1. Please find biblical examples of the use of each of the five kinds of power.

_____

_____

_____

_____

_____

_____

_____

_____

_____

_____

2. Please give practical examples from your experience of the use of each of the five kinds of power. If you cannot think of an actual instance, please describe a realistic potential one.

_____

_____

_____

_____

_____

_____

_____

_____

_____

3. What kind of power (or combination) do you *most* rely on – positional, coercion, reward, expert power or servant power?

_____

_____

_____

4. If you gave the original evaluation sheet regarding kinds of power to your spouse, friend or coworker, what would they say about the kind of power that you most rely on?

_____

_____

_____

5. What specific changes in your leadership do you need to make?

_____

_____

_____

_____

_____

_____

chapter 4

The Transformational Nature of Leadership

The first four kinds of power that we studied in the previous chapter (coercive, reward, positional and expert) all involve *exchanges* of some kind:

> **Coercion:** if you follow me, I won't punish you.
> **Reward:** if you follow me, I will reward you.
> **Positional:** if you follow me, you will be and feel legitimate.
> **Expert:** if you follow me, you'll end up in the right place.

But the final kind of power does not involve any exchange. It is a different kind of power: servant power is *transformational* power.

The more traditional leader has been called a "transactional leader" or an "exchange leader." The basis of transactional leadership is a transaction or exchange process between leader and follower. The transactional leader motivates his constituents by appealing to their self-interest. He provides for the meeting of his followers' needs and desires in exchange for them meeting his objectives. For example, political leaders exchange jobs, subsidies, and lucrative government contracts for votes and campaign contributions. Business leaders exchange pay and status for work effort. Traditional religious leaders exchange performing social rituals (e.g., marrying, burying, doing the opening prayer at the baseball game) in exchange for their constituents giving them a salary, health benefits and a retirement account. Denominational leaders provide certain benefits and resources for their pastors in exchange for those pastors remaining loyal participants in the denomination.

At its heart, transactional leadership represents the following exchange: "You give me something and I'll give you something."

Transactional leaders concentrate on the present, are good at traditional management functions such as planning and budgeting, and generally focus on impersonal aspects of job performance. In certain contexts, transactional leadership can be quite effective. By clarifying expectations, leaders help build their followers' confidence. Furthermore, satisfying the basic needs of constituents may improve effectiveness or morale.

Transactional leaders excel at keeping things running smoothly and efficiently. They design an exchange system that brings stability to an organization as it continues along its course.

Transformational leaders, on the other hand, initiate the actions that change the course of the organization. These leaders also understand and attempt to meet the tangible needs of their followers, but they go beyond the mere exchange process by empowering and inspiring their followers to fulfill their highest potentials in the calling and purposes of God. Thus, while it is more complex than transactional leadership, transformational leadership is also considerably more potent.

Transformational leaders motivate followers to do more than they originally expected to do (or believed they were able to do) as they strive for higher goals.

Transformational leaders focus on intangible qualities such as the will of God, vision, shared values and ideas as they build relationships and enlist followers in the cause. They engage the full person of the follower.

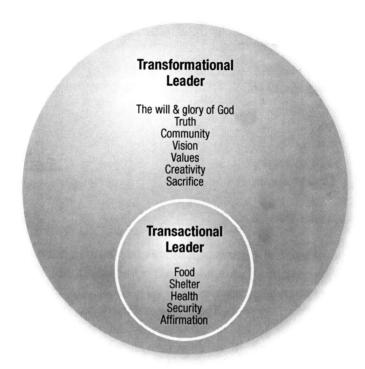

Whereas exchange leadership is characterized by coercion, reward, position or expertise, transformational leadership is characterized by integrity, creativity, communication, vision, passion and empowerment.

Thus, transformational leaders could also be called "servant" leaders, since their goal is truly to serve those they lead. Such a leader is not merely trying to fulfill his own purposes by using (or manipulating) other people, but he is genuinely serving the people. The servant leader's goal is that the highest potential of the people be fulfilled. His purpose is not merely the fulfillment of his own vision.

Transformation is radical change. To transform means to change in the way that a caterpillar transforms into a butterfly, or a tadpole into a frog, or a baby into a child and then into an adult, or the spring into the summer into the fall into the winter into the spring again. After the process is completed, it is as if the older form ceases to exist. Ice no longer resembles water after its transformation; steam no longer looks like water.

Servant leaders transform:

- People.
- Goals.
- Motivations.
- Organizations.

1. TRANSFORMATION OF PEOPLE.

Servant leadership develops followers into leaders. This is done by rallying constituents around a mission and defining the boundaries within which they can operate in relative freedom to accomplish the organization's goals. The people are motivated to take initiative and to solve problems. Such courageous leadership enables positive and pervasive change to happen, and is consistent with the true function of leadership: to produce more leaders, and not just more dependent followers.

2. TRANSFORMATION OF GOALS.

Transformational leadership seeks the highest. It is important for people's basic needs to be met through adequate wages, safe working conditions, and other considerations. However, the servant leader pays attention to each individual's personal needs for growth, development and fulfillment as the organization strives to accomplish God's will for everyone involved.

3. TRANSFORMATION OF MOTIVATIONS.

Unlike transactional leadership which focuses on "what's in it for me?", servant leadership inspires followers to go beyond their own self-interests for the good of the group. People are persuaded to do more than the bare minimum. Servant leadership motivates people to believe in the goals of the organization and to be willing to make personal sacrifices for its highest purpose.

4. TRANSFORMATION OF THE ORGANIZATION.

Servant leadership presents a vision of a desired future and communicates it in a way that makes the pain of achieving it worth the effort. Transforming visions engage people's commitment and launch them into action. Great things can be accomplished when people have a sense of divine purpose as well as a clear picture of where the organization is going.

Thus, in the local church context for example, transformational leaders develop "ministers" who are "called of God" to fulfill certain responsibilities while transactional leaders look for "volunteers." The following describes the difference:

> A volunteer looks at church meetings as another commitment he's been obligated to fulfill, but someone called of God looks upon meetings as another opportunity to be used by God.

> A volunteer looks upon any constructive criticism as negative, but someone called of God is grateful for feedback because he wants to be the best he can be.

> A volunteer puts in minimum effort, but someone called of God puts in maximum effort.

> A volunteer sits back and complains about this and that bothering him, but someone called of God leads a personal campaign to improve that which needs improvement.

> A volunteer feels threatened by the talent of others, but someone called of God feels secure in God's direction of his life.

A volunteer does no outside practicing or preparation (after all he's just a volunteer), but someone who is called of God strives to be as prepared as possible.

A volunteer wants to quit at the first sign of adversity or discouragement, but one called of God digs in and perseveres.

A volunteer is oblivious to the needs of his ministry, but someone called of God prays over the needs of his ministry.

A volunteer is more prone to jealousy of others, but one called of God praises God for distributing gifts and talents as He chooses.

A volunteer shrinks back from resolving relational conflict, but someone called of God seeks to resolve all relational conflict to preserve the unity of the team with which he serves.

A volunteer's main source of fulfillment is his talents and abilities, but someone called of God knows that being used of God is the most fulfilling thing you can do with your life.

A volunteer can't handle being put into situations where he's going to be "stretched," but someone called of God responds to God's call with humble dependence on Him.

This difference is reflected in the attitude of the leader himself: is he genuinely following the calling and vision of God or is he just doing a "job"?

How can you tell the difference between a job and a ministry? Some Christians merely have a job in the church. Others are involved in a ministry. There's all the difference in the world! How can you tell the difference between a job and a ministry?

If you are doing it because no one else will, it's a job. If you are doing it to serve the Lord, it's a ministry.

If you're doing it just well enough to get by, it's a job. If you're doing it to the best of your ability, it's a ministry.

If you'll do it only so long as it doesn't interfere with other activities, it's a job. If you're committed to staying with it even when it means letting go of other things, it's a ministry.

If you quit because no one praised you or thanked you, it was a job. If you stay with it even though no one seems to notice, it's a ministry.

If you do it because someone else said it needs to be done, it's a job. If you are doing it because you are convinced it needs to be done, it's a ministry.

It's hard to get excited about a job. It's almost impossible not to get excited about a ministry.

If your concern is success, it's a job. If your concern is faithfulness, it's a ministry. People may say "well done" when you do your job. The Lord will say "well done" when you complete your ministry.

An average church is filled with people doing jobs. A great church is filled with people involved in ministry.

If God calls you to a ministry, for heaven's sake (literally), don't treat it like a job. If you have a job in the church, give it up and turn it into a ministry! God doesn't want us feeling stuck with a job, but excited, fulfilled, and faithful to Him in a specific ministry.

Transformational leadership may be exhibited by anyone in the organization in any position, not only the top leaders. It may involve influencing peers and superiors as well as subordinates. It can occur in the daily acts of ordinary people, but it is not ordinary or common.

One of the ways you can discern a true divine call to leadership upon a man's life is by seeing if people are actually experiencing *transformation* through their interaction with him or if they are just getting things done.

> Leadership is not magnetic personality – that can just as well be a glib tongue. It is not "making friends and influencing people" – that is flattery. Leadership is lifting a person's vision to higher sights, the raising of a person's performance to a higher standard, the building of a personality beyond its normal limitations. (Peter Drucker)

1. Please think about the time of previous leadership success in your life that you discussed in chapter 2. Then answer the following questions:

    A. Was the leadership you exhibited primarily transactional or transformational? How do you know this?

    _____

    _____

    _____

    _____

    _____

    B. How could you have done it better?

    _____

    _____

    _____

    _____

C. Discuss your leadership experience (both how you actually did it and how you could have done it better) with regard to the following:

C1. People

_____

_____

_____

_____

_____

C2. Goals

_____

_____

_____

_____

_____

C3. Motivations

_____

_____

_____

_____

_____

C4. The organization

_____

_____

_____

_____

_____

2. Think of a leader you have known who was primarily transactional.

    A. How do you know he was a transactional leader?

_____

_____

_____

_____

_____

    B. What were the results of his leadership?

_____

_____

_____

_____

_____

3. Think of a leader you have known who was primarily trans-formational.

   A. How do you know he was a transformational leader?

   _____

   _____

   _____

   _____

   _____

   B. What were the results of his leadership?

   _____

   _____

   _____

   _____

   _____

4. In your small group, discuss your answers to the above questions together.

chapter 5

Three Kinds of Leadership

We can identify three broad kinds of leadership:

1. Authoritarian leadership. This is the leadership of the world that Jesus spoke about in Matthew 20:25.
2. Servant leadership. This is the leadership Jesus modeled and spoke of in Matthew 20:26-28.
3. Non-leadership. This is the leadership abdication that Peter tempted Jesus with in John 13:8. Such leaders generally withdraw from followers and offer little guidance or support. They are "leaders" in name only. This passivity may be the result of laziness, discouragement, intimidation[14] or personal weakness.

The following table contrasts the various behaviors of these three kinds of leaders.

---

[14] Some leaders are intimidated by strong power groups in the church, others by their own wives!

Leadership Behaviors

Authoritarian Leader	Servant Leader	Non-Leader
Promotes own personal vision	Aligns vision with followers' needs and aspirations	Has no clear vision
Self-serving vision	God- and follower-serving vision	Possesses no overarching purpose
Sets goals individually	Involves people in goal setting	Allows people free rein to set their own goals
Insensitive to followers' needs	Desires to meet followers' needs	Only responds to followers' needs when absolutely necessary
Uses power for personal gain or impact	Uses power to serve others	Uses power only when necessary for short-term advantage
Uses a combination of positional, coercive and reward power	Uses primarily servant power – sometimes some expert power	Often relies on positional power to maintain role
Engages primarily in one-way, downward communication	Engages in two-way, open communication	Engages in non-committal, superficial communication
Controls discussion with people	Facilitates discussion with people	Avoids discussion with followers
Demands own decisions be accepted without question	Stimulates followers to think independently and to question the leader's view	Lets others make the decisions unless he has a vested interest in it
Censures critical or opposing views	Learns from criticism	Ignores criticism, if possible
Threatened by independent thought from a follower	Encourages and praises independent thought from a follower	May be positive or negative toward independent thought by a follower

Authoritarian Leader	Servant Leader	Non-Leader
Sets policy and procedures unilaterally	Solicits and receives input regarding the determination of policy and procedures	Allows people to set policy and procedures
Dominates interaction	Focuses interaction	Avoids interaction
Hoards information to maintain control	Dispenses information to empower others	Ignores information if possible
Micro-manager	Strategic manager	Non-manager
Personally directs the completion of tasks	Provides suggestions and alternatives for the completion of tasks	Provides suggestions and alternatives for the completion of tasks only when asked to do so by people
Rarely delegates entire projects – only small parts – so he maintains complete control	Strategically delegates entire projects to develop the people doing them, as well as to get the job done	Does not delegate, but rather "dumps" entire projects on others
Gives over-explicit directions on every project he "delegates"	Gives strategic direction – balances getting the job done right with developing the person and allowing for new and different ideas	Gives little direction
Takes advantage of others for the benefit of his own vision	Coaches, develops and supports followers	Leaves others alone unless asked to get involved
Demands all recognition	Shares recognition with others	Allows others to take recognition
Provides infrequent positive feedback	Provides frequent positive feedback	Provides infrequent feedback of any kind

Authoritarian Leader	Servant Leader	Non-Leader
Focuses on negative behavior	Focuses on positive behavior while dealing appropriately with the negative	Ignores as much as he can
Rewards obedience and punishes mistakes	Rewards good work and uses punishment only as a last resort	May offer either rewards or punishments
Is a poor listener	Is a good listener	May be either a poor or good listener
Uses conflict for personal gain	Mediates conflict for corporate gain	Avoids conflict
Acts more like a parent in a dysfunctional family	Acts like a leader in a healthy organization	Acts more like an abstainer from duty
Negative role model	Positive role model	Negative role model

The Effect of Leadership Style on the People

The research shows that leadership style has a significant impact on the people:[15]

1. Non-leadership and servant leadership styles are not the same. People with non-leaders are not as effective or fulfilled as people with servant leaders. Under non-leaders, people generally have a feeling of isolation and they withdraw from participation in the group. One exception to this is the highly-motivated and expert person who may do well under a non-leader.

2. Although groups led by authoritarian leaders are often the most efficient, servant leaders also achieve high – and considerably more stable – efficiency. People under authoritarian leaders only maintain high effectiveness when the leader is present. Moreover, such leadership enhances performance

---

[15] See *Leadership: A Communication Perspective* (2nd ed.), by Hackman & Johnson, pp. 32-43.

on simple tasks but decreases performance on complex tasks, such as birthing an entirely new vision or subunit of the organization.

3. Groups with authoritarian leadership experience more hostility and aggression than groups with servant or non-leader leaders. Hostile and aggressive behavior in the form of arguing, division, and blaming occurs much more frequently in authoritarian than in other groups.

4. Authoritarian-led groups may experience discontent that is not evident on the surface. Moreover, such groups will experience a very high turnover rate of people.

    One church had an extremely authoritarian leader but seemed, outwardly and superficially, to be in unity. However, after the leader had died, severe division erupted and eventually destroyed the church. This division had always been there – under the surface – but everyone had been too afraid of the leader to rock the boat.

5. People exhibit more dependence and less initiative under authoritarian leaders. People in authoritarian groups will appear more submissive than those in other groups. They will be less likely to initiate action without the approval of the leader, and less likely to express their opinions and ideas than people in other groups.

6. People demonstrate more creativity and innovativeness under servant leaders.

7. People exhibit more commitment and cohesiveness under servant leaders. They have a stronger sense of responsibility to the group, will be more committed to the group's vision, and will be more supportive and friendly toward each other.

The following is an adaptation from one of Aesop's Fables:

The frogs wanted a leader. They began to search for the leader of their dreams. One of them found a log and brought it back to the pond, and, for a while, the frogs were happy with their new leader.

Soon, however, they found out they could jump up and down on their new leader and run all over him. He offered no resistance nor even a response. The log did not have any direction or purpose in his behavior, but just floated back and forth in the pond. This practice exasperated the frogs, who now decided they needed "strong leadership."

Abandoning their log-leader, they went back to their search for a leader. Finally, one of them found a stork and persuaded him to return to the pond and be the frogs' leader. The stork stood tall above the members of the group and certainly had the appearance of a leader.

The frogs were quite happy with their new leader. Their leader stalked around the pond making great noises and attracting great attention. Their joy turned to sorrow, however, and ultimately to panic, for, in a very short time, the stork began to eat the frogs!

The frogs were like some church members who go from one extreme to the other!

Variables

It should be noted that the extent to which a true servant leader will either centralize authority in himself or give authority away may sometimes vary depending on the circumstances. Some variables are:

- Culture.[16] In certain cultures, leaders are expected to be more "authoritarian." The servant leader may look a little different in such cultures, but will still be a *servant* leader.
- The level of maturity of followers. Paul's leadership style would, no doubt, have been different in a new church that had just been planted, compared to his style in an older, more mature church. He would have been considerably more directive in the baby church. Nevertheless, he would always have been a true servant.

---

[16] Certain cultures can also predispose people towards certain abuses.

- The level of maturity needed for a particular situation. In certain situations, the people will not have sufficient skills or maturity to exercise appropriate leadership. At this point, the leader may step in and gently "take over." Nevertheless, his spirit and motive should always be that of the servant leader. Accordingly, he will not merely make the right things happen, but he will work primarily to develop the people to be able to do it themselves next time.

Servants or Bosses?

A Christian leader should not be the "boss" of those he leads. A boss:

- Is "in charge."
- Maintains strict control over others by directly regulating policy, procedures and behaviors.
- Creates distance between himself and others as a means of emphasizing role distinction. He often does this by a variety of symbolic means, using titles, clothing, and other status symbols.
- Believes that the people cannot function effectively without his direct supervision.
- Tells others what to do and always how to do it.
- Is the one to get permission from to do everything.
- Constantly looks over everyone's shoulders to see what's happening, or if they're doing everything "right."

Instead, there is mutual respect and trust in the relationship between a servant leader and his followers.

In another book,[17] we will examine leadership that is so authoritarian it becomes abusive.

---

[17] Please see *Abusive Leadership: SpiritBuilt Leadership #6* by Malcolm Webber.

EXERCISE

1. Which kind of leadership – authoritarian, servant or non-leader – do you respond to most favorably?

    _____

2. Why do you prefer this particular style?

    _____

    _____

    _____

3. Which kind of leadership – authoritarian, servant or non-leader – do you typically exhibit?

    _____

4. What exactly do you do that is characteristic of this kind of leadership?

    _____

    _____

    _____

5. What are some specific ways in which you could improve your leadership style? Please be *specific*; don't simply say, "I need to be more of a servant."

_____

_____

_____

_____

_____

_____

6. What can you do to encourage others – your superiors, coworkers and subordinates – to adopt the leadership style you prefer if they don't currently exhibit that style?

_____

_____

_____

_____

_____

_____

chapter 6

Senior Pastors and Leadership

Many senior pastors serving churches today are not truly leaders, although they hold a position of leadership.

Research by George Barna among senior pastors of Protestant churches in America has shown that:

- Less than one out of every ten senior pastors can articulate what he believes is God's vision for the church he is leading.
- Only five percent of senior pastors say they have the gift of leadership. Most pastors think they were neither called to nor divinely equipped for that task.
- The typical pastor works long hours (more than 60 hours a week), but devotes less than 10 hours a week to specific leadership activities.[18]

The traditional pastor is essentially a spiritual "care-taker" (a spiritual manager) of the people he serves. He visits the sick, marries the young people, buries the old people, and is there for every need.[19]

Interestingly, two-thirds of all adults and more than nine out of ten Protestant senior pastors say they are leaders. As Barna observes:

Leadership has positive connotations in our society and therefore people want to be associated with it. Unfortunately, "leadership"

---

[18] See *Today's Pastors* by George Barna.
[19] Please see *Leaders & Managers: SpiritBuilt Leadership #5* by Malcolm Webber.

has become such a misused, misunderstood and generic word that most people and behaviors are now subsumed under the term's umbrella. It's similar to what has happened with terms such as "Christian," which 85% of [American] adults call themselves, even though half of those people admit that they have no relationship with Jesus Christ, or "evangelistic," a label embraced now by almost nine out of ten churches even though most of them have not seen a new convert in the past year. "Leadership" has befallen the same definitional elasticity.

We recently interviewed more than 2400 Protestant pastors and discovered that 92% of them said they are leaders. Then we gave them the definition that we use of leadership and saw the proportion drop to less than two-thirds. When we then asked if they felt that God had given them one of the spiritual gifts that relates to leading people, such as leadership, apostleship or even administration, the proportion plummeted to less than one out of four. Finally, we asked them to dictate to us the vision that they are leading people toward – that is, the very heartbeat of their ministry – we wound up in the single digits.

Our surveys also revealed that less than 2% of Senior Pastors believe they are doing a "below average" job of leading their congregations, a figure that is "unrealistically low." Pastors who consider themselves to be leaders are most likely to defend that belief on the basis of saying they do an "excellent" job in teaching and in encouraging people. While those are worthy and much-needed skills, they have little to do with a person's calling to lead a group to fulfill a God-given vision. The surveys found that most of the pastors who deem themselves to be leaders ranked themselves comparatively low on attributes such as mobilizing people to pursue a vision, accumulating the tangible resources needed for that pursuit, and providing people with clear direction based on the nature of the vision. Those were some of the characteristics we categorized as central to effective leadership.

Several pastors expressed their concern that concluding that most pastors are not called by God to be leaders reflects an anti-pastor bias. However, this research does not criticize the heart or ministry of pastors; it simply affirms that they will have their most positive effect through the exercise of other gifts and offices. Pastors are good people, well-educated and called to ministry, but perhaps not to the ministry of leadership.

Unfortunately, churches have created a ministry model that expects the pastor to be gifted and skilled in an unrealistically diverse and large number of areas. I have not said that many of today's pastors should not be in ministry, but simply that we have set them up for failure by expecting them to be something that God Himself hasn't called them to be. Ideally, pastors who are not called to be habitual leaders can be released from the responsibilities of leadership and instead focus on what they are gifted at and have been called to, and partnering with people whose ministry is primarily that of leadership.[20]

Leadership Is Different From Teaching

As noted above, many of today's pastors are, in reality, teachers.

- They say they enjoy teaching and preaching the most.
- They are called and gifted by God to teach.
- They spent years in seminary or Bible school developing their abilities to exegete the Scripture and to share its truths.

Today's confusion between the role of teaching and the role of leadership has made it difficult for many pastors, who are trained and gifted to teach, to understand why they are ineffective in facilitating progress toward the achievement of a God-given vision. They are excellent teachers but their churches are not moving forward!

---

[20] See *A Fish Out of Water* by George Barna.

Certainly, a man can possess both leadership and teaching giftings, but we must understand the great differences between the two.

Leaders	Teachers
Influence through vision and personal example	Influence through ideas and words
Provide direction and motivation	Provide intellectual challenge
Seek corporate transformation	Seek individual growth
Love to strategize	Love to study
Need a core of committed and impassioned followers	Need a teachable audience
Make decisions	Teach the truth
Motivate people to action	Motivate people to think

The Need for Leadership

These are great days of restoration in the church of Jesus Christ. Peter prophesied that a profound and far reaching time of "restoration" would come before Jesus' return:

> Repent, then, and turn to God, so that your sins may be wiped out, that times of refreshing may come from the Lord, and that he may send the Christ, who has been appointed for you – even Jesus. He must remain in heaven until the time comes for God to restore everything, as he promised long ago through his holy prophets. (Acts 3:19-21)

The twentieth century was known as the "Century of the Holy Spirit" as God poured out His Spirit in a wonderful way upon the earth. But there is much restoration to go. The church herself must change – she must become more like the organic "bride" and "body" of the New Testament.

For this to happen, there must first be a restoration of leadership. We will never experience the joy and fruitfulness of New Testament church life without first the reestablishment of New Testament leadership.

Paradigms and Paradigm Shifts

A "paradigm" is a mental model that describes a particular view of the world. It is a set of rules and regulations that defines boundaries and provides a means for being successful within those boundaries.

A "paradigm shift" is a revolutionary change. When a paradigm shifts, the success of the past becomes less relevant, because the criteria for success have been altered and new standards established. The victories of the past no longer apply to the present or future. The rules change, the roles change, and the definition of success changes. Everyone goes back, however temporarily, to a lower point on the learning curve. In profound paradigm shifts, everyone goes back to zero and begins to learn all over again.

The church is undergoing profound changes in our day. Many are positive changes brought about by the Holy Spirit, and reflecting returns to a more biblical style of church life and leadership. A few, however, are negative. Some of these changes are summarized in the following table.

The New Realities for Church Leadership	
Old Paradigm	**New Paradigm**
Tradition	Relevance
Stability	Change
Control	Empowerment
Competition	Collaboration
Autonomous Ministries	People and relationships
Privileges	Responsibilities
Credentials	Performance
Faithfulness	Effectiveness
"Prepared" for ministry	Lifelong learners
Preaching	Ministry strategies
Leader is key	Team is key
Leaders are born	Leaders are made
Closed door	Open book
Infallibility	Honesty
Avoid failure	Take risks
Good management	Good leadership
Individualism	Community
We "go to" church	We "are" the church
People as spectators	People as participants
Narrow comparison	Broad comparison
Theory	Experience
Uniformity	Diversity
Need- & duty-based ministry	Gift- & calling-based ministry

Old paradigm: Tradition is central.
New paradigm: Relevance is central.

Yesterday's spiritual leaders were judged on the basis of how closely they followed the "hallowed traditions" of whatever group they were a part of – whether or not their ministry ever impacted anyone's life. Today it is considerably more important that they are able to lead a ministry that is relevant and transforming.

Old paradigm: Stability is cherished.
New paradigm: Change is valued.

Today's world is in constant motion, being characterized more by disorder than by order. It is vital that the church change to stay relevant in a fast-changing world. In the past, many leaders assumed that if they could just keep things running on a steady, even keel, the church would be successful. Their goal was that the church be an oasis of unchanging spiritual tranquility in the midst of a turbulent world. In reality, however, change is inevitable in church life. The church is a living organism, and living things grow and change. If there is no change it means there is no growth, and if there is no growth it means the church has died. It actually takes more energy to try to make things stay the same than to accept the inevitability of constant change and recognize change itself as a potential source of energy and increased fruitfulness.

Old paradigm: Leaders control.
New paradigm: Leaders empower.

Spiritual leaders once thought the people needed to be told what to do, why to do it, how to do it, when to do it, how long to do it for, and who to do it with. They believed that strict, central control was necessary for the church or organization to function efficiently and effectively. Rigid organizational hierarchies, structured jobs and work processes, and detailed, inflexible procedures let everyone know that those at the top had power and those at the bottom had none. Today's leaders, however, share power rather than hoard it, and find that by giving power away they are actually increasing the organization's effectiveness by getting everyone involved and committed. By empowering people through giving them genuine responsibility along with the authority to fulfill that responsibility, servant leaders become power-generators for the church or ministry.[21]

Old paradigm: Leaders compete with each other.
New paradigm: Leaders collaborate with each other.

The move to empowerment also ties into new ways of leading that emphasize collaboration over competition and conflict. Within churches and Christian organizations, teams and other forms of collaboration are eliminating the old model of individuals competing with each other for ascendancy. In addition, there is a growing trend toward breaking down barriers and increasing collaboration with other churches and ministries, as we recognize that, in reality, we are all on the same team working for the same Lord toward the same goal. Instead of competing with each other for the affiliation of the saved, leaders should compete with the world, the flesh and the devil for the attention of the lost.

Old paradigm: We must build autonomous ministries.
New paradigm: We must build relationships.

The increase in collaboration both within and among churches and Christian organizations reflects another fundamental change: a shift from an emphasis on autonomous ministries to an emphasis on relationships. In the past, leaders were concerned with building their individual "ministries." Today the long-term relationships they have with other leaders and people are more important than a ministry that may change or disappear entirely in a short time when its purpose is fulfilled.

---

[21] Please see *Leading: SpiritBuilt Leadership #3* by Malcolm Webber.

Old paradigm: A position of leadership brings privileges.
New paradigm: Leadership brings responsibilities.

Under the old paradigm, people sometimes competed with each other for recognition as leaders because they wanted the privileges that came with the position: salary, nice clothes, respect, titles, and the freedom to enjoy a largely undisciplined lifestyle. Today, leadership effectiveness is not only expected but demanded, bringing with it a greater burden of spiritual responsibility.

Old paradigm: Credentials are very important.
New paradigm: Performance is very important.

Yesterday's leader relied much more on positional authority. He held the degrees and the title; therefore, he was in charge and people followed him. Many times a certain degree was considered a bare minimum qualification for a leader. Today, many successful leaders have no degrees at all. Moreover, many people do not care about credentials as long as the leader is doing a good job of leading. Additionally, those with degrees and titles who are not consistently performing will face increased pressure to change or to leave.

Old paradigm: Faithfulness is sufficient.
New paradigm: Effectiveness is expected.

Faithfulness means loyalty, showing up on time, hard work, and not complaining about your poor pay or conditions. But that is not enough today. Today you must also know what to do when you show up on time, and you must get it done before you leave. It's not that a lack of faithfulness is acceptable today, but simply that it is no longer sufficient. You must also be effective; you must accomplish. Moreover, you must accomplish continually. What have you achieved recently?

Old paradigm: Spiritual leaders are "prepared" for ministry.
New paradigm: Spiritual leaders are lifelong learners.

In the past, being a "spiritual leader" involved a limited set of ministry skills that included visiting the sick, marrying couples, burying the dead, visiting the elderly, taking care of the church building, overseeing the finances, representing the church at community functions, and preaching a good, biblically-sound sermon on Sunday. This limited set of skills could be learned in a few years in seminary. Now, however, a world and church environment that is constantly changing demands not only that leaders learn new things but that they do so continuously, and that they do so with breakneck speed. Yesterday's skills will not keep up with today's demands and certainly not with tomorrow's.

Old paradigm: Preaching is more important than ministry strategies.
New paradigm: Ministry strategies are more important than preaching.

This shift is not so much that preaching has decreased in importance, but that appropriate ministry strategies have greatly increased in their comparative importance. Preaching used to be the primary attraction to a church and the main function of the leader. This is why a spiritual leader used to be addressed as "Preacher," and was jokingly accused of working for only one day (or even one hour!) a week. While preaching is still vitally important in a healthy church, the spiritual leader also needs to be heavily involved in leading the multitude of ministry strategies that comprise the life of today's church. Moreover, he is no longer the one-man show he used to be, but has become the leader of an extensive team of ministry leaders involved across the life of the church. The importance of ministry strategies is seen in the fact that, in some churches, some of the key ministry leaders may never preach a single sermon in their lives yet are directly responsible for many aspects of the spiritual life and health of the church.

Old paradigm: Ministry in the church depends on the leader.
New paradigm: Ministry in the church depends on the team.

Since today's church has greatly increased in complexity, no one person is able to do it all; it takes a team to build a church. Under the old paradigm, the pastor was the key player in the church with his name on the church sign. Any other leaders operated under him merely as his extensions. Today's leadership team consists of strongly gifted and dedicated men and women, each of whom shares primary leadership responsibilities. Thus the senior leader has become more of a team builder and coach than the old one-man show he used to be.

Old paradigm: Leaders are born.
New paradigm: Leaders are made.

The old "silver-spoon" theory of leadership taught that leaders must have had the correct lineage and been endowed from birth with the look, personality, and sensibility of power and authority. Today we recognize that leaders are both born and made. Consequently, leadership is not only within the reach of a few specially "gifted" people. Moreover, since many leadership skills can be learned and improved upon, people at all levels in our organizations are expected to develop in leadership.

Old paradigm: Closed-door leadership.
New paradigm: Open-door leadership.

In the past, leadership decisions would be made behind "closed doors," the people not being party to the issues nor to the process, many times. Then the leaders' decisions would be announced to the people. Today the people want to know what is happening, and often demand to be a part of the process – at least in some measure. Moreover, effective servant leaders actually invite the people to be involved in the process.

Old paradigm: Leadership is infallible.
New paradigm: Leadership is honest.

Closely related to the shift from closed- to open-door leadership is the shift from leaders presenting themselves as largely infallible (or at least fairly close to it) to leaders being very honest with the people. Such leaders are known as "real people"! In the past, the leader would be afraid to acknowledge his own personal weaknesses or his uncertainty about what he is doing, due to his fear that the people would reject him. Today the leader who refuses to acknowledge his humanity is more likely to be rejected as "phony."

Old paradigm: Failure is to be avoided at all costs.
New paradigm: Take risks and learn from failure.

Under the old paradigm, we believed that a spiritual leader should never fail. Consequently, when leaders made mistakes they would be hidden, swept under the rug, denied, or the blame passed on to others. Moreover, risk should be avoided. Under the new paradigm, leaders know that just because they fail it does not make them failures. In fact, they realize they must be willing to fail in order to ultimately succeed. Consequently, they take risks and learn from failure.

Old paradigm: Good management makes successful churches.
New paradigm: Good leadership makes successful churches.

Yesterday's paradigm assumed that if we have efficient management, produce short-term results and streamline the process, we will be successful. Today, good management is not enough. We must also have effective leadership that will make the necessary changes and establish world-changing vision.

Old paradigm: The church is a collection of individuals.
New paradigm: The church is a living community.

Yesterday's leader was content to minister one-on-one to people as a random assortment of individuals who were essentially disconnected to each other, except for an occasional superficial coming together. Today's leader is building a living spiritual community that exists all week long – 24 hours a day, 7 days a week. This is considerably harder to accomplish. Moreover, it requires a whole new vision and an entirely different set of skills!

Old paradigm: You "go to" church.
New paradigm: You "are" the church.

In the old paradigm, success meant that the Sunday morning program went well. Today, success and failure are understood in terms of the lives, relationships and ministries of the saints all week long – 24 hours a day, 7 days a week. It is no longer enough to put on a successful religious "performance" once a week. Today's churches are never "closed."

Old paradigm: The people are spectators.
New paradigm: The people are participants.

The old model of church had the pastor doing all the praying, preaching, building maintenance, visitation, etc., while his wife played the organ, arranged the flowers, and cooked for the "pot-luck" dinner! Meanwhile everyone else looked on. Today's model recognizes the imperative of Ephesians 4:11-16. Every member is a minister, and the primary responsibility of the leader is not to do the works of the ministry, but to equip the people so that they can do them.

Old paradigm: Success is defined by narrow comparison.
New paradigm: Success is defined by broad comparison.

In the past, most pastors were rated by their people according to how they compared either with their predecessors or with a few other pastors in town. Today the field of comparison is much broader. Because of televised religious gatherings, the increased mobility of people from town to town and church to church, and the wide availability of spiritual ministry through books, tapes and seminars, today's church leaders are compared to hundreds of others. People do not make these comparisons consciously but they do make them. This raises their expectations for their own leaders and places much greater stress upon those leaders. This is not particularly fair, but it is a reality nevertheless.

Old paradigm: Theory is sufficient.
New paradigm: Anything less than an experience will not suffice.

In the past, it was sufficient for the leader to know and state theories of spirituality. Today, people are searching for an experience. It is no longer enough simply to believe the right things; people want to know God.

Old paradigm: Uniformity is valued.
New paradigm: Diversity is valued.

Past models of church growth have promoted the "Homogeneous Unit" as the key principle of evangelism: people who think alike, act alike and look alike will be the most effective in reaching people like themselves. This strategy has intentionally produced churches in which everyone is either the same, or similar – in color, age, income, social standing, etc. Certainly, it is true that homogeneous groups find it easier to get along, communicate and understand one another. Our world, however, is rapidly changing, becoming increasingly multicultural. Moreover, in Christ, God has broken down the walls of partition between the races (Eph. 2:14), genders, and social classes – we are all one in Christ (Gal. 3:28) and that reality should be reflected in our churches. Thus, while the Homogeneous Unit Principle (HUP) is effective in evangelism, a single homogeneous unit is not appropriate as the total expression of the local church community.

Old paradigm: People minister according to the need and according to duty.
New paradigm: People minister according to their gifting, calling and preparation.

There will be times when we have responsibilities and duties to fulfill, whether we think we're "gifted" in that particular area or not. However, the overall context of our churches must be *gift-based* ministry. Or, we could describe this more properly as *calling-based* ministry.

God has given every member of His church a calling. He was the One who set every member in His church, and He has given each one a purpose to fulfill – not only to receive from the ministry of others, but also to give. When we all give, when we all function, then the body grows to maturity.

> *From him the whole body, joined and held together by every supporting ligament, grows and builds itself up in love, as each part does its work. (Eph. 4:16)*

Moreover, God has given every believer the giftings to fulfill his calling. Thus, when a believer functions according to his calling and giftings, then he will be doing it in the power of the Holy Spirit – not just his own strength – and then, together, the church will accomplish the impossible!

When a believer functions according to his calling and giftings, he will not only be more successful in what he does but he will also be more fulfilled. He'll be blessed because he's doing what God has called him to do. Consequently, he won't burn out.

Traditionally, however, the pastor dictates what needs to be done in the church and exactly how it should happen, and then he tries to find "volunteers" to do it for him. When no one volunteers, then the pastor applies pressure – usually guilt: "If you don't teach Sunday School for the next 6 months, who will?" This results in lots of square pegs in round holes – guilty pegs at that!

The traditional approach starts with the task and then tries to force people into that mold. The biblical approach, however, starts with the person and says, "Who are you? What is your calling from God? What are the gifts He's given you to fulfill that calling? And how can we help you to build a place in the church in which you can fulfill that calling?"

The biblical approach starts with the person and then the ministry comes from them. This results in more round pegs in round holes!

These and other similarly profound changes have caused many "old school" leaders considerable pain and disequilibrium as they have tried to understand and embrace the new paradigm.

chapter 7

A Lack of Leaders

In the church today we have many wonderful shepherds (spiritual managers) and teachers. However, we lack leaders (Matt. 9:36).

Today's Spiritual Management-Leadership Mix			
		Leadership	
		Weak	Strong
Management	Strong	Too many	Almost none
	Weak	Too many	Too few

So, what is the solution?

Certainly, the solution is not to diminish the roles of the shepherds and teachers. God has called all of us to certain responsibilities and He has gifted us in specific ways so that we all have a vital part in the building up of His body.

The solution is not to banish teachers and shepherds from the church. There are thousands of godly, faithful spiritual managers who have poured out their lives in the service of God's people and who need to be commended and encouraged for their work. They should, however, be released from their specifically "leadership" responsibilities if they are not gifted or called to fulfill those functions. Additionally, leaders must be raised up who will lead the church into the purposes of God. Finally, our structures must allow them to lead.

Additional books in this *SpiritBuilt Leadership* series address these issues.

Books in the *SpiritBuilt Leadership* Series

by Malcolm Webber, Ph.D.

1. *Leadership.* Deals with the nature of leadership, servant leadership, and other basic leadership issues.

2. *Healthy Leaders.* Presents a simple but effective model of what constitutes a healthy Christian leader.

3. *Leading.* A study of the practices of exemplary leaders.

4. *Building Leaders.* Leaders build leaders! However, leader development is highly complex and very little understood. This book examines core principles of leader development.

5. *Leaders & Managers.* Deals with the distinctions between leaders and managers. Contains extensive worksheets.

6. *Abusive Leadership.* A must read for all Christian leaders. Reveals the true natures and sources of abusive leadership and servant leadership.

7. *Understanding Change.* Leading change is one of the most difficult leadership responsibilities. It is also one of the most important. This book is an excellent primer that will help you understand resistance to change, the change process and how to help people through change.

8. *Building Teams.* What teams are and how they best work.

9. *Understanding Organizations.* A primer on organizational structure.

10. **Women in Leadership.** A biblical study concerning this very controversial issue.

11. **Healthy Followers.** The popular conception that "everything depends on leaders" is not entirely correct. Without thoughtful and active followers, the greatest of leaders will fail. This book studies the characteristics of healthy followers and is also a great resource for team building.

12. **Listening.** Listening is one of the most important of all leadership skills. This book studies how we can be better listeners and better leaders.

13. **Transformational Thinking.** This book introduces a new model of transformational thinking – of loving God with our minds – that identifies the critical thinking capacities of a healthy Christian leader. In addition, practical ways of nurturing those thinking capacities are described.

Strategic Press
www.StrategicPress.org

Strategic Press is a division of Strategic Global Assistance, Inc.
www.sgai.org

2601 Benham Avenue
Elkhart, IN 46517
U.S.A.

+1-574-295-4357
Toll-free: 888-258-7447

CPSIA information can be obtained at www.ICGtesting.com
Printed in the USA
LVOW070539171012

303188LV00001B/11/P